ABER

Essays on Aberystwyth ◦ **Photos by Keith Morris**

Gomer

Published in 2008 by Gomer Press, Llandysul, Ceredigion SA44 4JL
www.gomer.co.uk

ISBN 978 1 84323 940 6

A CIP record for this title is available from the British Library

This book is published with the financial support of the Welsh Books Council.

Printed and bound in Wales at Gomer Press, Llandysul, Ceredigion

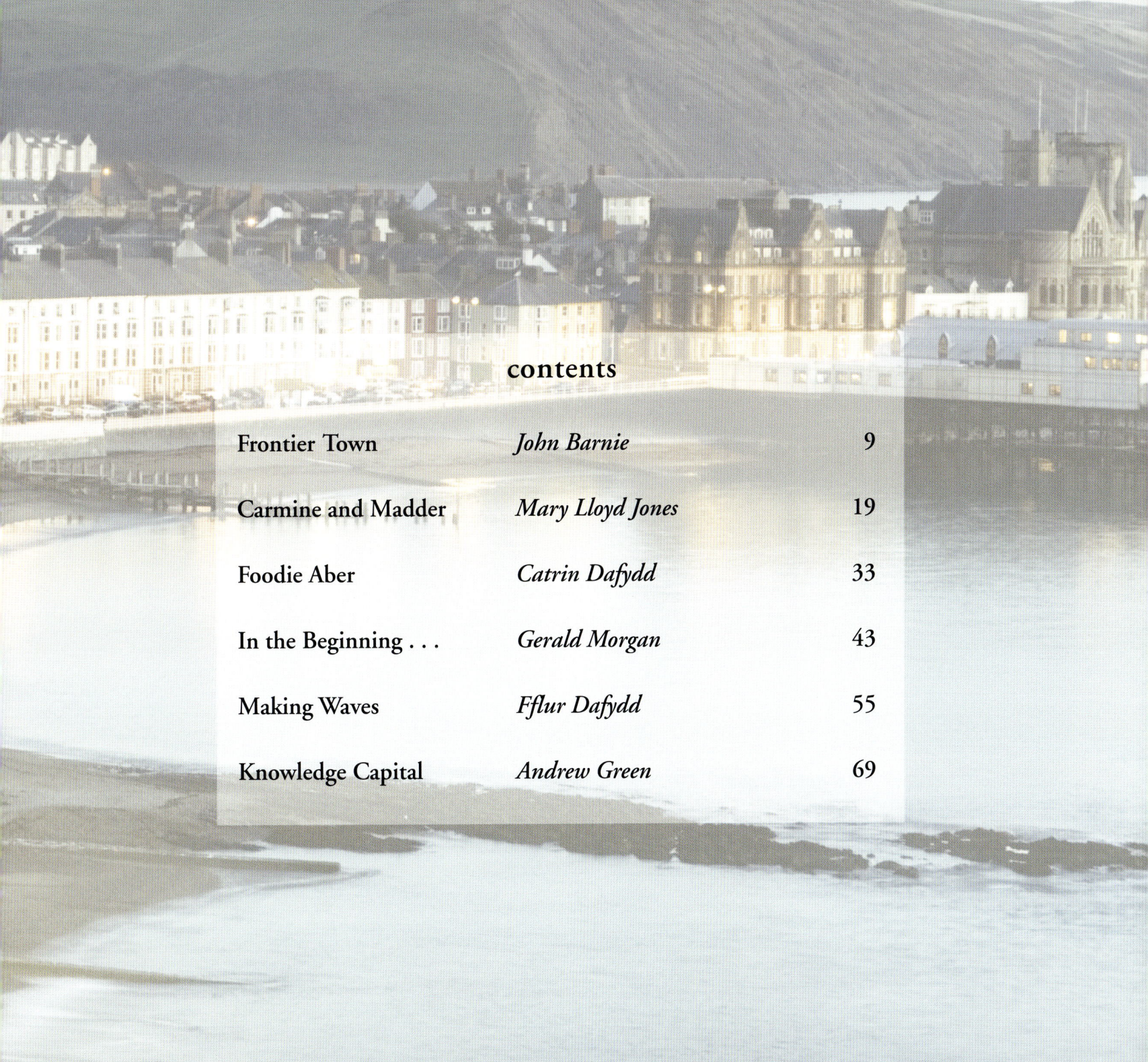

contents

Frontier Town

John Barnie

In the 1950s railway posters advertised Aberystwyth as the place 'Where Holiday Fun Begins', inviting you to join happy family groups frolicking on the town's golden sands. There must have been many a day-tripper from the Midlands who, grasping the Promenade railings, looked down in disbelief at the curve of grey grit and black rock that in fact constitutes the Aberystwyth foreshore. Yet in many ways the beach that exists is far more interesting than the sands of the poster painters' imagination, for its dull-looking surface hides a multitude of life forms that is one of the town's great riches, even though most people who visit – and many townspeople, too – will be unaware of it.

One of the pleasures of living in Aberystwyth is that within its small compass you can find experts on almost anything, who are willing to give up their time and share their knowledge with you. Go to the intertidal rock pools by the Pier with zoologist Willie Sinclair, for example, and you see them in a new and revealing light. The glistening rock looks unpromising from the Promenade, but make your way across it at low tide and you realise that the 30 degree dip in the strata creates hundreds of pools, each of which is a kind of sea garden teeming with life.

As you approach a pool, a prawn may scuttle out of sight under overhanging seaweed; common limpets are clamped like tiny outcrops of the rock itself; a hermit crab the size of a fingernail makes its way across a pool floor with an old periwinkle shell on its back. Picked up, it retreats into the shell, so all that can be seen is its one outsized claw defending the entrance. Flat periwinkles graze on their typical food, the serrated bladder wrack, while in one pool, unusually, they spread across a meadow of sea lettuce, the normally drab molluscs sporting vivid orange shells and bodies which contrast strikingly with the seaweed's almost luminous green.

The intertidal pools are harsh environments. In summer they heat up and suffer oxygen depletion; in winter they can be colder than the surrounding sea as the tide retreats. The creatures of the pools must adapt to this. They are dangerous places in other ways, too, for many of the inhabitants. The dog whelk is one of the great predators of the pools, settling on a mussel or periwinkle and softening up a small area of shell with enzymes before drilling a tiny hole with a tongue-like apparatus set with backward-facing teeth. When the hole is drilled, it stuns its prey with poison before devouring it. The hole is so perfectly round it looks as if it has been machine-tooled.

Aberystwyth's tidal pools are home to a variety of seaweed species. Bladder wrack dominates the mid-tidal zone, its lush, glistening swathes combed into patterns this way and that by the retreating tide, as if the land artist Andy Goldsworthy had just passed by. You can find the olive-coloured *Fucus erratus* anchored to suitable rock, and knotted wrack in more sheltered locations. These are the seaweeds remembered from childhood holidays. Also common to the pools is *Corallina officinalis*, an attractive pinkish plant that branches profusely, with a calcified bead at the end of each 'twig'. Exposed as the tide retreats, its heavy head lolls on the rock or bends into the pool below. *Lithophyllum incrustans* is another pink-coloured seaweed found here and there, encrusted, as its Latin name implies, on the rock.

It is easy to believe that the intertidal pools are more or less unchanging, but nature is never static. Twenty years ago, the beautifully named snakelocks anemone was not easily found among the rocks by the Pier; now it can be seen in small colonies in the deeper pools, the clusters of khaki-green tentacles looking like exotic, fleshy

plants. It has the unusual feature of not being able to retract its tentacles like the common sea anemone and is prone to drying when exposed to the air for any length of time. It is usually found therefore below the waterline of the pools.

After an afternoon stumbling over the rocks, peering at the intense, small-scale life of the pools, it is a shock to climb back up the steps to the Promenade and walk along Terrace Road, merging with the bustle of the town's human world. What is familiar seems, for a moment, strange, as if part of you is still there with the hidden creatures of the foreshore on the town's frontier with the sea.

Explore Tan-y-bwlch with Arthur Chater, botanist and former Keeper at the Natural History Museum, London, and another aspect of this frontier comes into focus. Walking along the canalised bank of the Ystwyth in winter, Tan-y-bwlch can seem a bare, exposed place with little of interest. But again if you bend low you will see the wide variety of plants, a number of them rare, that have established themselves in this seemingly hostile environment. Sea campion, sea mayweed, sea plantain, sea pink, curled dock, tree mallow, herb robert, water dropwort, Ray's knotgrass (named after John Ray, the great seventeenth-century English naturalist), sea purslane, sea rush, sea holly, sea poppy, goosefoot, can all be found there – each with its specialised niche along the embankment, or in the harsher conditions of the pebble and gravel beach. Perhaps one of the strangest is a rare, prostrate blackthorn growing between the embankment and the river. It presents a thick tangle of branches and thorns like common blackthorn, but it grows to barely eight inches above the ground. Tests have shown that this low growth is a genetically inherited trait, and that all the bushes on the sea side of the Ystwyth are in fact one plant, linked underground by its root system. There is also evidence to suggest that the plant is old; perhaps two hundred years or so.

If more were needed, the Aberystwyth shoreline is rich in bird life, with choughs, wheaters, rock pipits, stonechats and whinchats all visible within twenty minutes walk of the town centre. Purple sandpipers, that breed high in the tundra of the north, can be seen in winter among the rocks, as well as rare wanderers like the Mediterranean gull, and even accidentals from North America such as the laughing gull, blown here across the Atlantic on westerly storms.

At Tan-y-bwlch it is less easy to ignore the fact that Aberystwyth sits on a restless frontier. The River Ystwyth, diverted from its natural course in the eighteenth century to join the Rheidol in the harbour, will, if left to itself, eventually burst its canalised banks and enter the sea at the south end of Tan-y-bwlch. Then the pasture land it runs through will revert to salt marsh. There is an argument that it should be allowed to do so because the marsh would act as a natural flood buffer for the town, absorbing some of the effects of spring tides as global warming leads to stormier weather conditions and a relentless increase in sea levels later this century.

The pebbles at Tan-y-bwlch and at Ynys Las north of the town are an indicator of other momentous changes. The pebbles derive from a wide variety of rock types, some having been driven by longshore drift over many millennia from cliffs to the south; others, originating in Ireland or the north of Scotland, were brought to the area as glacial debris during the last Ice Age. They are a reminder that Aberystwyth, which sits so sedately behind its sea wall, is only here for the short term.

Eight thousand years ago – the twinkling of an eye in geological time – the frontier between land and sea was some fourteen miles to the west in what is now Cardigan Bay. But progressive melting of the ice sheet and glaciers at the end of the last Ice Age redrew the border, the sea encroaching further and further on the land to the east, drowning young forests of Scots pine, birch and oak as it advanced, and forcing Neolithic hunter-gatherers to retreat to higher ground. The legend of Cantre'r Gwaelod, the Lowland Hundred, must have been born then; the story of the drowned towns and villages of Cardigan Bay becoming embellished over the centuries as folk memory of the environmental catastrophe was passed on from one generation to the next.

The remains of the drowned forest of the Cantref can be seen at low tide at the south end of Tan-y-bwlch, at Clarach, and most spectacularly at Borth where the stumps of pine and oak, and sometimes whole trunks of fallen trees, appear and disappear with the shifting of the sands at each tide. It is hard to imagine that people lived in that forest, moving among its trees under grey cloud or in dappled light, where now the mackerel glides.

It would be fascinating to return in five or ten thousand years. Perhaps there will be no Tan-y-bwlch then, but a salt marsh alive with ducks and waders, with ospreys and sea eagles, herons and egrets, looked down on by the long-abandoned Iron Age ramparts of Pendinas. North along the coast, Borth will perhaps have joined the villages of Cantre'r Gwaelod beneath Cardigan Bay, and tales about it will be told by the inhabitants of the seaboard town of Machynlleth, perched on the edge of the Bay's eastward extension into the Dyfi valley.

Below Pendinas there is the site of a Mesolithic tool manufactory. When I visited it with Arthur Chater, he bent down and soon found a microlith, a tiny stone tool, or part of a compound tool, characteristic of the Mesolithic period 12,000–3,000 years ago. Yet we know next to nothing of the hunter-gatherers who worked there, neither the name of their tribe nor what language they spoke, looking out over the shelving land to the west where, as the Ice Age ended, new-growth forest sprang up, only to be inundated later by the rising waters of the sea.

For now, though, we are here, and Aberystwyth's sea wall holds the waters at bay. Each summer the tourists come: the day trippers and caravan dwellers; the wet-suited surfers; the anglers, hands in pockets, rods balanced on tripods, watching their lines disappear into the waves. Few will notice the gorgeous orange hues of the flat periwinkle in the rock pools by the Pier, or think anything much of the low-lying blackthorn at Tan-y-bwlch if they pass it by. Nor for that matter will most of us who live here, though the periwinkle and blackthorn are each part of the almost inconceivable wealth of the town.

I would like to thank Willie Sinclair for sharing with me his knowledge of the marine life of the Aberystwyth rock pools, and Arthur Chater for introducing me to the rich flora and fauna of Tan-y-bwlch.

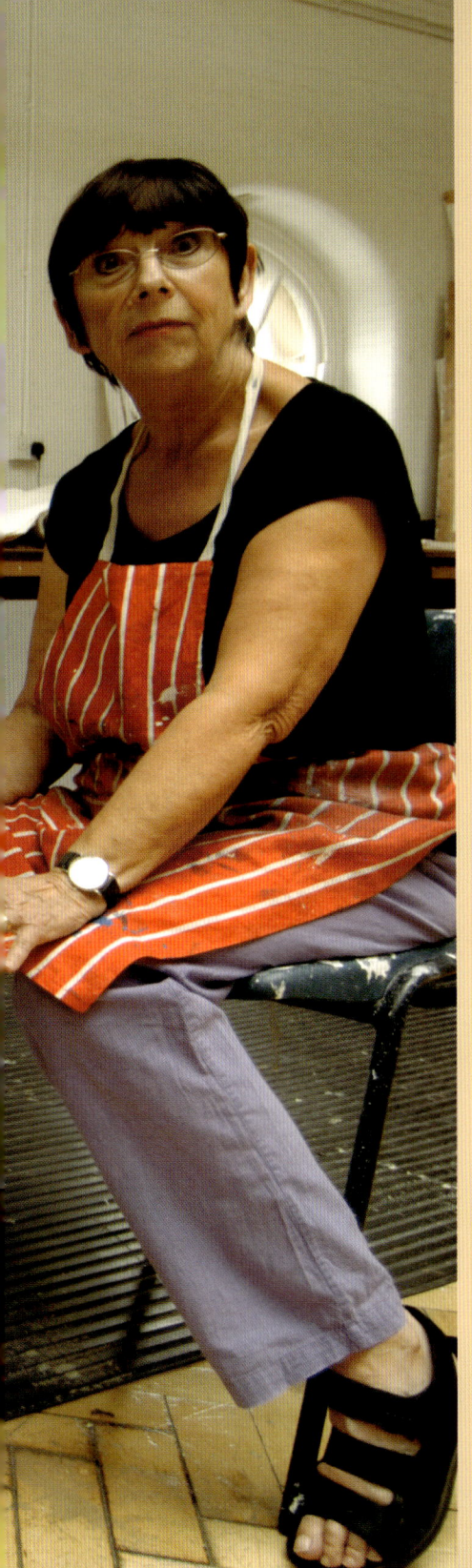

Carmine and Madder

Mary Lloyd Jones

In our densely populated islands of Britain, relatively remote places to the north and west are deemed generally disadvantaged compared with the south-east. Mainstream, centrist media journalists will sometimes mention Aberystwyth, comparable with Siberia, as a destination to be avoided: to leave the centre of civilisation for a place off the map will obviously never be a good career move.

This attitude has resulted in this small town being given a totally undeserved negative image. For its size – a population under 20,000, including 7,500 students – Aberystwyth has more thriving cultural institutions than one would find in many much larger towns and cities. The exceptional quality of life enjoyed at all levels has until now been a very well kept secret. No other town or city in Wales can compete with continuous programme of theatre, lectures, concerts, film festivals and exhibitions offered by the publicly funded establishments; I refer here to the National Library of Wales, the University, the School of Art, Ceredigion Museum and Aberystwyth Arts Centre.

Life in Aberystwyth is convivial; the whole town is walkable, so on my way to my studio, to the shops or to have a blow on the prom, my walk is interspersed with vigorous conversations and unplanned encounters. Being bilingual, I move from

Welsh to English and back unconsciously. I have pondered whether there is a difference in the first exchange in either language. I have come to the conclusion that the first words in Welsh usually take the form of a bit of leg-pulling and a few jokes – Ceredigion people are known for their wit. One of the hazards of traversing Great Darkgate Street is to find your way blocked by a clutch of raucously laughing farmers. A stronghold of the Welsh language, Aberystwyth is also a multilingual, cosmopolitan community where Polish, Urdu, Chinese and Japanese are all tolerated and respected.

In many ways, this is very like a small French town. The intense dramatic exchanges of French housewives on their morning expeditions to market is replicated in the conversations heard in the Tree House organic shop or Ultracomida delicatessen. With several excellent restaurants and independent food shops – and with some help from global warming – we are developing a café culture. This is the result of the enterprise of the owners of establishments like the Orangery, Blue Creek, the Olive Branch and again the Tree House providing congenial surroundings where friends can meet to drink good coffee and eat locally sourced healthy food. With four publicly funded galleries, attending private views is a regular opportunity to meet fellow spirits. In addition to a large number of practising artists, the audience for exhibitions includes art historians, curators, art teachers and, increasingly, collectors of art.

Unlike many other towns, Aberystwyth has maintained the character of its town centre with buildings of architectural merit interspersed with Victorian and Edwardian terraces. No motorway has been carved through the centre and so far we have been spared large-scale demolition. We can learn from France and Italy where great pride and interest is taken in the architecture of the built environment and the will is there to restore and preserve, as opposed to the rampant demolition which is such a characteristic of urban Britain.

To appreciate the rich variety od styles in the streets and terraces of the town it is necessary to focus on the details. The porches, doorways and windows of houses in Park Avenue, Alexandra Road, Stanley Terrace and Penglais Hill, for example, are truly a feast of exuberant invention. Here, in the houses that have maintained their

character, we have variety and unity of design. The houses, with few exceptions, are well maintained and painted in a joyful interaction of colours. Individual buildings deserve attention: the Bangor Garage in Park Avenue in stylish red brick, the simple facade of the Salvation Army building in Alexandra Road and the magnificent Art Nouveau window of the Black Horse Pub in Portland Street. At present we have an architectural heritage that we can enjoy and which contributes greatly to the wellbeing of all who can use their eyes.

My fear is, however, that philistine forces are waiting to destroy what exists and that too many fail to appreciate the wealth of good buildings in Aberystwyth. My fears are well placed as we must now live with the result of past mistakes. The splendid town clock, built in 1859, was demolished only to be replaced with what is known as the Noddy clock. The Kings Hall, a splendid 1920s Art Deco building, was demolished to be replaced by flats of depressingly banal design and a gap – like a missing tooth – in the sweep of the promenade. Shop fronts with Victorian and Edwardian details almost weekly disappear, destroying the unity of design. Several of the shops in Terrace Road still have mosaic doorsteps, all unique, but sadly the majority have been obliterated. A special project, giving schoolchildren or students an opportunity to photograph architectural details, leading to an exhibition to celebrate the built environment of Aberystwyth would be a good idea. Would this be enough to alert the population to a disappearing asset?

The recently published master-plan drawn up for Aberystwyth is a worrying document, advocating amongst other things an increase in retail facilities. The forces of globalisation and the power of multinational chains, unless opposed on a local level, could spell the destruction of small independent shops which are the life force of a small town like Aberystwyth, and an economic demise would surely mean the loss of fine buildings as well. Architectural gems that need to be treasured and protected are too numerous for a comprehensive list here, but here are a few: the Old College on the promenade, the Carnegie Library, the Post Office and all the town houses in Laura Place and some in Bridge Street. The School of Art is special; donated by the Davies sisters of Gregynog originally for the use of the university's

chemistry department, it is unique. With its graceful staircase (simply asking for a dramatic entrance), its black and white marble floor and highly polished brass door knobs, and the parquet floors of the studio, ensure that as a school of art it is outstanding. Order is maintained amongst traditionally anarchic and messy art students – they are made to wash their hands! – and the building as a workplace demonstrates the uplifting effect of good architecture.

The intelligence needed to understand and enjoy, for example, the intricacies of *cynghanedd* should be easily transferred to the reading of architecture. Going back to the Greeks, understanding the language of architecture is to do with proportion and measurement, with the relationship between subdivisions and the whole. Every successful building is the result of unity of concept and attention to detail. In Aberystwyth at present, the evidence points to a general indifference to the subject of architecture and to a lack of knowledge of the successive styles from classical through Georgian, Victorian and Edwardian that can be seen in the buildings of this town.

Housing in Aberystwyth is built on the wooded hills surrounding the harbour and sea front. This mix of woodland interspersed with housing creates a particularly enjoyable environment. The blessing of a large number of mature trees cannot be underestimated. Yet, I have witnessed the felling of magnificent specimens and there is increasing evidence that this destruction continues. The depressing conclusion is that what we have inherited is undervalued.

Next to Hay on Wye, Aberystwyth is a good destination for book lovers. Everywhere independent bookshops are closing, yet this small town supports four second hand shops in a total of thirteen bookshops.

When so much of value is drowned in celebrity culture and dumbing down, it is refreshing to realise that in Aberystwyth, scholarship and learning is respected and appreciated and is a natural part of the culture. As is the case in France, to be an intellectual here is not an embarrassment. In addition to the university, the twin towers of learning on the hill, the National Library and the Centre for Advanced Welsh and Celtic Studies, offer an extensive programme of lectures, seminars, exhibitions and debates which are invariably well attended. Early booking is needed

to secure a seat in the popular five o'clock lectures on highly specialised subjects, for example 'The 15th-century Poets of the Nobility', or 'Iolo Morganwg and the Romantic Tradition in Wales'.

Facing west towards Ireland, exposed to wild seas and spectacular waves, an Aberystwyth resident's life is closely interwoven with the natural world. Those carmine and madder skies viewed from the National Library steps or the Arts Centre café and memories of levitation by the wind on the prom compel many to make return journeys to this corner of Wales. The daily drama of the elements make tangible that other world of shape-shifting caught in the tales of the Mabinogi, in the life of the ancient bard Taliesin, the sorceress Ceridwen and the submerged township of Cantre'r Gwaelod. When I view the unrelieved ugliness of much of the flat land occupied by large conurbations, I am thankful to live in a land that feeds the imagination, a land of undulating hills and steep valleys where the juxtaposition of light on a hillside and floating cloud shadows can generate a gasp of wonder.

As a painter, I consider that the hinterland to the east of Aberystwyth is my particular territory. The foothills of Pumlumon, the valleys of the Ystwyth, Rheidol and Mynach are my source material. This is a countryside of surprising variety, a treasured wilderness as yet little known. Walking amongst the remains of the old lead mines one rarely meets anyone. A land rich in minerals, deep gorges and an astonishing number of waterfalls, it is still relatively undiscovered. Being 'off the map' does not suggest prosperity, and yet unrestrained tourism has been a curse in many places. Nevertheless, all businesses in Aberystwyth and the surrounding area would benefit if more was known about the area and if proper control was in place for future developments.

In a fast-moving world of terrifying global forces, survival for those placed geographically on the margins is undoubtedly a challenge. Resisting change in itself is not an option. To avoid undesirable developments imposed from outside, however, initiatives for the future must come from the inhabitants of Aberystwyth. Identifying existing strengths will point the way to a possible future. The vigorous cultural life of the town indicates that adding to the existing facilities would be a sound use of existing skills and talents. Many role models exist of areas, towns and cities that have

been revitalised and transformed as a result of ambitious investment in the arts. The Guggenheim Museum in Bilbao, Kilmainham Hospital and Temple Bar in Dublin, and Tate St Ives are all stimulating places, as is proved by visitor numbers.

The phenomenal success of the Barn Centre in Aberystwyth, which existed for less than a decade in the 1980s, is a perfect model for the way forward for this town. The Barn Centre, an untidy complex of variously sized spaces vacated by the University, provided a dynamic cultural powerhouse where the buildings were used to house studios and performance spaces for theatre, dance, film and media projects, photographers, painters and musicians. Many leading, successful arts practitioners in Wales had their first opportunity to develop their careers in the Barn Centre.

Plans by the university to vacate the Old College on the seafront have caused dismay. But could this apparent disaster be an opportunity for history to repeat itself in a positive way? This splendid Gothic pile could house a reborn Barn Centre with room for a version of a National Gallery. Aberystwyth and the surrounding area is home to a large population of creative artists; an ambitious transformation of the listed Old College would be one way to give Aberystwyth a deserving place on the cultural map of Britain and preserve its treasures for future generations. As Raymond Williams said in *The Long Revolution*, 'It is through art that society expresses its sense of being a society. The artist in this is not the lonely explorer, but the voice of his community.'

ICE CREAM
HUFEN IÂ

Cone
£1.10

With
a
flake
£1.25

waffle cone
£1.50
with a flake
£1.75

Foodie Aber

Catrin Dafydd

A female foodie's take on Aber – from Art Centre salads to rissoles from the chippy; Aberystwyth, a digestive microcosm of life.

It strikes you, as soon as you've left the place. I don't think it can strike you unless you've left the place. I thinks that in the leaving lies the parting, and the possibility of coming back to muse on what has been. What has been, and what cannot be again. That which will not come back, that which one would not care to recreate. The recreation that would only alter the exactness of what has been. The exact and proper mess of life. Its ups and its downs, its faltering moments and its exhilarating ones too.

Picture the scene. A mouthful of hummus with coriander oozing from every chickpea pore. Green and cream, on a silver fork. Look down at the plate now. Copious amounts of red cabbage and fennel seeds, sultana-speckled salad and fabulous looking new potatoes covered in olive oil, basil and bits and bobs. One lonely tomato sits there too. The Arts Centre salad was a favourite of mine. As you looked out from the campus concourse, your eyes sliding down towards the wide, panoramic view of the sea, this salad made you feel as if you had arrived. You were also often in good

company; your closest friends surrounding you. Soon, another Mocha would entice you. You were in no rush.

Picture the scene. A rissole, one of life's unsung delicacies. Given to you, hurriedly, by a dear friend. Your mascara's streaming. Too much gin. Your hair's in your mouth. Eat it, she says. Eat it, you'll feel better. He isn't worth it, wasn't worth it. Those awful nights, when *y felan** is visiting. Those nights when not even the sea, not even a walk up Consti, or even a cheeky Martini in The Pier will mend your broken heart. You're sensitive to others' grief too. As you walk, in a zig-zag-head-down-don't-let-anyone-see-me-like-this fashion, from town up to the halls of residence, you are a detector of raw emotion. Spot the girl who leaves the club with her ex-boyfriend. Spot the dog looking for its dead owner. Spot the loss in the barman's eyes as he sucks on his fag-break fag. Spot the strange goings-on on the corner near Spar. Spot the homeless person who looks at you angrily. I think he owns this street by now. I daren't tell him that this street isn't his. Not in Aberystwyth, and certainly not tonight.

On my return visits here, memories come alive. Vivid memories of the highest ups one has ever experienced, and unsolicited memories of the lowest lows. Aberystwyth seems to allow all of life to live within its walls. Everything has been, and will be, experienced here. The sheer enormity of life's experiences will take place here, in this quaint little town.

The Chicken Tikka Masala Lasagne –
  Aberystwyth; a place for experimentation
Picture the scene. Two girls creating a horrid concoction. Jars of tikka-masala sauce, roast chicken, fried onions, lasagne sheets, béchamel sauce. Oh yes, and cheese. A combination of Italian and Indian with a pinch of Welsh cuisine flair. That is the beauty of

* Y felan – Welsh for depression or perhaps the blues in this case.

Aberystwyth, or at least the beauty of being a student at Aberystwyth. You're left to your own devices, and you're allowed to experiment. As it turns out, the lasagne was delicious (unlike many a monstrosity – I say monstrosity because some of the creations seemed to take on their own lifelike qualities) and housemates dribbled in jealousy as we ate, and ate.

Being creative in Aberystwyth is nothing out of the ordinary; it is the natural thing to do. Trying your hand at a few new tasks is made easy, and failing at something can become equally as easy to deal with.

I was interested in experimenting at Aberystwyth. Not, as it turns out, with drugs, but rather with writing and politics. Aberystwyth is a place that allows you to question and criticise and become your own person. It is a place obsessed with itself and inherently obsessed with the world, in equal measures. Sometimes seeming like the centre of the world (much as you tend to feel in London after staying there for a while) and at other times feeling as if it hasn't a single link with the world outside. Its internationality penetrates your being, and yet, the big blue sea reminds you that you are in a little town in Ceredigion, at the edge of land and at the beginning of the unknown.

This intensity can sometimes become overwhelming, especially in terms of political or artistic experimentation. But that intensity can also be the sweetest tasting toffee that you've ever placed on your tongue. Once you learn the rhythm of Aberystwyth, you will learn to take its eccentricities in your stride.

Actual Diary Insert: *'Cyfarfod Eleri ar ôl darlith ôl-foderniaeth. Coffi a Brownie'* (Meet with Eleri after post-modernism lecture. Coffee and Brownie).

Often, discussing Derrida and a future boyfriend (hopefully) over a mocha becomes a common occurrence for a student in Aber. The idea that you can down tools and enjoy a discussion about a lecture that you've just attended is made possible by a generous amount of study time encouraged by the University.

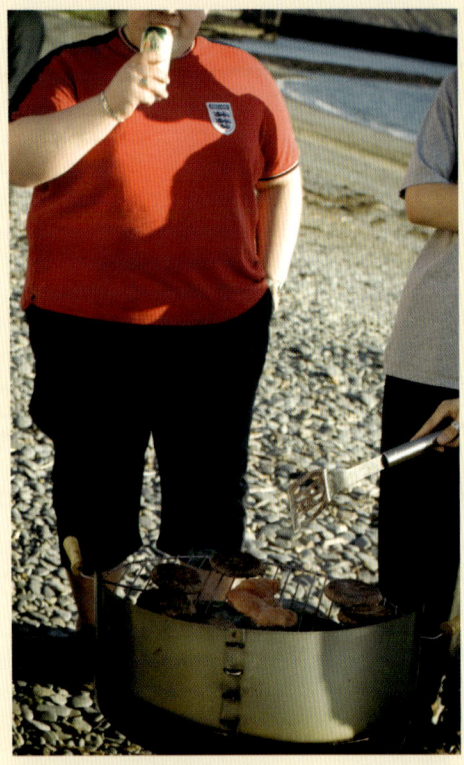

Having been raised in Gwaelod-y-garth, between Pontypridd and Cardiff, I hadn't understood that people in some places sat in cafés drinking tea at any time of day. I was given to believe that time had a more orderly, structured framework. There is something of the Irish in the Aberystwyth lifestyle.

Choosing which café to visit, which soup to slurp, which library to frequent, which module to study, makes Aber a place of decisions. But, above all, it is a place of possibilities. Its size as a town makes one feel as if anything is possible, all is within one's grasp, and suddenly one's made acutely aware of a responsibility to steer a course and make important lifestyle choices. Aberystwyth allows one to realize that one can control the pace at which one's life moves. I doubt if there are many places left in Wales where that can be said to be true.

A spoonful of Marmite

Eccentricities are accepted in Aber, if not over-celebrated, and so my nightly unscrewing of the yellow Marmite lid was seen amongst my friends as nothing less than a necessity.

It strikes you, as soon as you've left the place. I don't think it can strike you unless you've left the place. I thinks that in the leaving lies the parting, and the possibility of coming back to muse on what has been. What has been, and what cannot be again. That which will not come back, that which one would not care to re-create. The re-creation that would only alter the exactness of what has been. The exact and proper mess of life. Its ups and its downs, its faltering moments and its exhilarating ones too.

Leaving Aber is similar to leaving home before arriving at Aber. In Aber, you see the world and its issues from a very different perspective. Leaving Aber, and being given time to contemplate its effect on you, is similar to the experience of looking at the world from Aber. Only that one thing has changed. You will only ever be a visitor from now on. Driving through, stopping for ice cream or meeting friends. You'll be a visitor even if you stay for a whole week. As much as you might try, you cannot re-

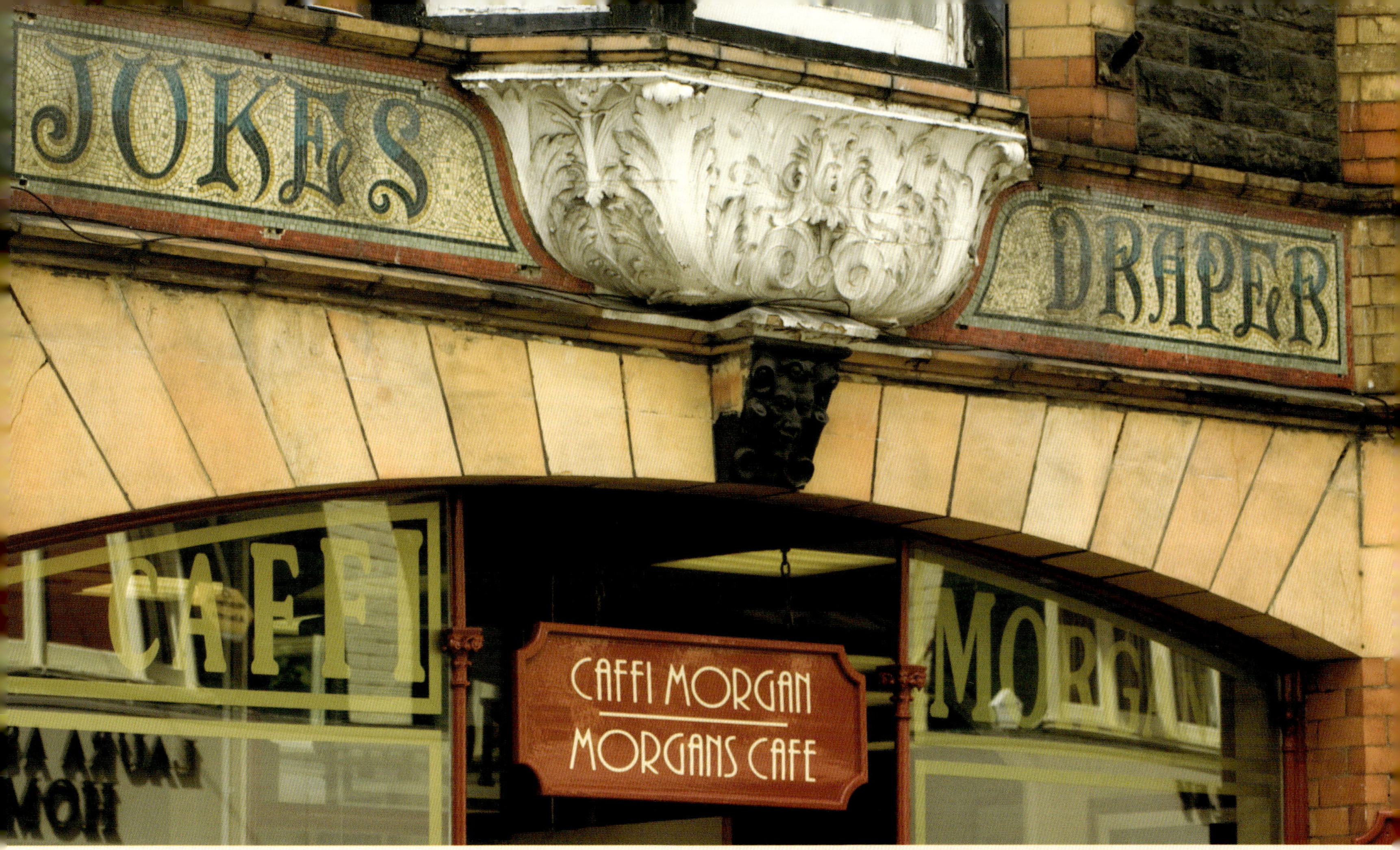
JOKES
DRAPER
CAFFI
MORGAN
CAFFI MORGAN
MORGANS CAFE

eXpress
FISH AND CHIPS

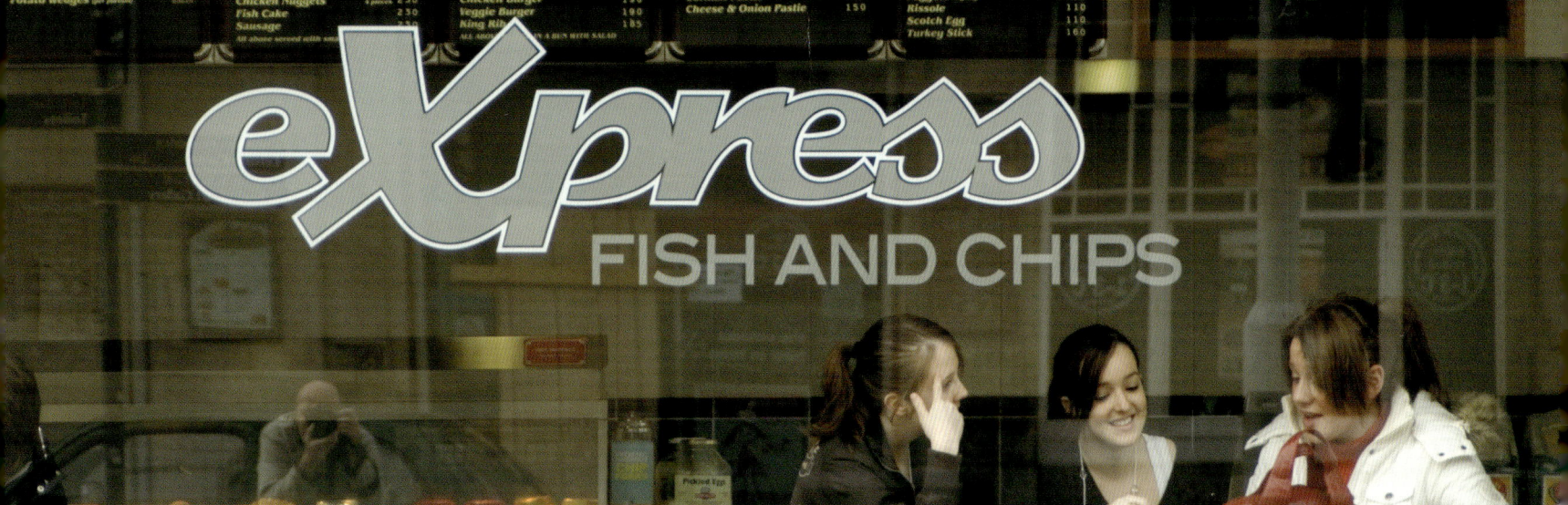

capture the experience of living there although you sometimes catch a glimpse of the memories if you tune in carefully. Not just memories, but the essence of the emotion you felt way back when. The actuality is hurled back from the living, breathing bricks of the town. But don't get drunk on those memories, because they'll soon disappear again and leave you standing in a seaside town, trying to decide which café to visit. Trying to fall into the Aber lilt in a matter of hours is a trap into which I have fallen, and it fails without exception. But you'll always try and get into the groove again. You just can't help it, although you know damn well that it isn't a place you can visit; rather, it's a place where you must be.

In the beginning . . .

Gerald Morgan

If you look around you, signs of Aberystwyth's beginnings are there for you to see, but not in the mighty hillfort of Pen Dinas which was abandoned over a thousand years before the town began. Rather its roots lie in the fine ringwork castle crowning the hill above Llanychaearn, best viewed from the Ceredigion Coast Path above Tan-y-bwlch, also visible in winter from the A487 at Rhydyfelin. Built in 1110, this first Aberystwyth was fought over fiercely between English and Welsh, but when Edward I conquered Ceredigion in 1277 he built a new castle with borough on the north bank of the Rheidol, and the name Aberystwyth mysteriously attached itself to his new town.

You can also see the borough's simple plan. The medieval streets are still there like ghosts, though buried under tarmac: the main street from the castle to the Great Dark Gate in the north-east, the cross street from the bridge to the Wig, the rocks where the pier now stands. Look up and down Great Darkgate Street and you can see, in the frontage of the shops, the plots or burgages which were divided and rented out to the town's first burgesses. Even the ghostly line of the town wall can be followed, though every stone has gone; down by Baker Street, along Chalybeate Street and then back to the castle via Mill Street. All those names are themselves ghosts of the later past of the town.

But who were the men and women of early Aberystwyth? We know the names of the bigwigs whom Edward appointed to office in Aberystwyth: constables of the castle like Roger de Molis, Bogo de Knovill, Robert de Tibetot and John Scudamore. These were Edward I's servants, but also men who owned lands elsewhere in Wales and beyond Offa's Dyke, holding many offices under the crown – they can't have been seen here very often. We are nearer to our local ghosts when we encounter Geoffrey Clement.

It's true that Geoffrey was a man with wide responsibilities in south-west Wales. He was an administrator and, when necessary, a warrior, who was rewarded by Edward with extensive lands in Pennardd (near Strata Florida) and Genau'r-glyn; he must have lived in the castle when helping to strengthen it in 1287. He fought against the Welsh rebels of 1287 and again in 1294, when he met his death. His widow Margery had taken refuge in the castle, but once the rebellion was over, she laid claim to her husband's lands, and those of other men too, and held a burgage in Aberystwyth which may have been this doughty woman's home. Moreover she was granted income from a share of the fines in the local courts, the medieval equivalent of a state pension.

How do we know that Margery Clement held a burgage in Aberystwyth? Because a list of the burgesses of Aberystwyth survives from the year 1301. This fascinating document tells us that Aberystwyth had twice the population of Caernarfon, and in population nearly matched Conwy, which Edward had at first intended as his capital in north-west Wales.

So who were the burgesses of Aberystwyth in 1301? There are 112 names in the list, only five of them women. Knowing as we do how Edward had conquered Wales, how his northern boroughs had only English burgesses, it is a surprise to find that 51 of the Aberystwyth burgesses have Welsh names, while some are obscure. Moreover they held an appropriate share of the town land, some 40%. The Englishmen were most often known by the places from which they had come to west Wales: Thomas of Lichfield, Adam of Wigmore, John of Pederton in Somerset, Vincent of Hilton in Huntingdon, Robert of Chard in Somerset, Richard of Redesdale in Northumberland.

Other men with apparently English names had come from elsewhere in Wales – Roger of Ystrad Dewi and John of Cemais, both safe men from Pembroke, along with Philip of Carmarthen. There was also a William Scot, who perversely may have been Irish.

Several men are known by their occupations: William Janitor, Robert Carpenter, Robert Faber the smith, John Clericus, probably a man with humble office in the Church. William le Plumer – was he an arrowsmith, or simply a plumber? Others have nicknames as surnames: Richard Careless, Richard Gobiond and the splendidly named John and Robin Gotobedde, a name which still survives in East Anglia.

Then there are the men who are clearly Welsh, either from their patronymics – Richard ap Thomas, David ap Iocyn, Philip ap Meurig – or their nicknames, Madog Cwta, Henry Cam, John Goch, Ieuan Sais. These nicknames are intriguing: Cwta was presumably a stumpy fellow, Cam may have meant 'squint-eyed' rather than crooked, while Ieuan Sais was no Englishman, but a man who knew English, probably having spent time beyond Offa's Dyke. Ieuan Chwith would have been left-handed. Philip ap Nest and Hugh ap Gwerfil were like Twm Sion Cati in later years, named for their mothers, but whether or not they were, like Twm, illegitimate, cannot be known.

Most of the burgesses held one burgage each, but some held more; a total of five men – three of them Welsh – held three burgages, and William or Gwilym Gam held four. In contrast John Scudamore, constable of the castle, was modestly content to possess two burgages. As one would expect, only a handful of women held property: Angharad gwraig Hubert Cam, and Gwenllian gwraig Morris (?) were clearly Welsh, Petronella gwraig Howel may have been Welsh, Agatha presumably English, along with Margery Clement, whom we have already met. Perhaps we should add the mysterious name of Dwys to the list of women tenants, and it is possible Mold Morgan would be known to us as Mallt or Maud.

One of early Aberystwyth's wealthiest men was William Cam, who held four burgages. It's his name that is intriguing. In its Welsh form, Gwilym Gam, this is the name of the father of Dafydd ap Gwilym. That is not in itself proof that this man and Dafydd's father are one and the same. Nevertheless, we know that Dafydd's paternal

ancestors held land on the king's behalf in north Ceredigion, which could explain our man's four burgages. Moreover, in another document to be described in a moment we find the rare female name Erdudfyl, which we know was the name of Dafydd ap Gwilym's mother. It might seem that the coincidence of having the two names in documents for the same period was too much, and that Dafydd's parents really did live in Aberystwyth or the immediate area – and tradition tells us of his home at Brogynin, near Penrhyn-coch.

Even more interesting than the list of burgesses to anyone who wants to put real people back into early Aberystwyth is a set of papers in the National Archives at Kew which have never been published. These are papers listing fines paid by dozens of men and women in the reeve's court for Llanbadarn, i.e. Aberystwyth.

The document is a list of every man and woman brought before the local reeve's court who has had to pay a fine because of some minor offence. Unfortunately most of the offences are not named; most entries simply say, for example, 'William Cam for the complaint of David ab Wele', or 'Ieuan ap Robin for a certain trespass'. Most of the fines are sixpence (wages for a day or two) or less, but whatever Ieuan ap Robin's offence was, he had to pay 13 shillings and fourpence – a mark, or two-thirds of a pound. That was a serious fine. One odd case is that of Richard ap Meredith who in seven successive courts was fined threepence 'for the pledge of Adam of Wigmore'. What on earth was going on?

Some offences are named. Several men were fined for selling fish on the seashore 'contrary to the statute of the town'. There were strict rules about who could buy and sell; men paid for licenses to trade in the town and the countryside around, and would have been keen to uphold the statutes. Ieuan Mab Tal was fined a shilling for trading illegally in the country. Other named offences were of a kind we might expect: David ap Philip paid 2s for having wounded Ieuan ap Tegwared, and Christiana daughter of Robert paid sixpence 'for the shedding of blood', but whose blood we are not told. Two individuals were fined on separate occasions for 'raising the hue and cry', the equivalent of a false 999 call today. Women were not afraid to complain against men: Alice daughter of Walter successfully brought William the

Chaplain, no less, before the court, though as usual the nature of the complaint is unknown. Roger the Carpenter was fined sixpence for threatening the bailiff.

The number of people fined is quite extraordinary for such a small community. During the winter of 1302-03 no fewer than 114 people paid fines, mostly at the complaint of a named individual. That doesn't mean that there were 228 people involved; a number of those fined were also complainants. But since the adult population of the town cannot at the most have been more than three hundred, visits to court were frequent.

A number of men who are named as burgesses in the first list also appeared before the court to complain or to pay fines. One of the town bigwigs was William the Janitor. We know from other records that he was the castle janitor or porter-cum-caretaker, and that he was something of a crook, having been punished for stealing eight flitches of bacon, presumably from the castle stores. No wonder that he was able to pose as one of the two most propertied burgesses in the town – he paid rent for four plots. He was in trouble in the local court for selling fish without a license, and for calling the reeve a thief. William's wife Lleucu and his servant Madog were both fined twice at the complaint of others. William may have been an Englishman but he had certainly found a Welsh wife.

A matter of particular interest is the number of women named in the court register of fines as either plaintiffs or accused. We meet Matilda the Nurse – probably a wet-nurse. We meet the unnamed wife of Moelgoch ('bald-red') who complained against Alice of Cemais; Hunydd daughter of Rees, Gwenllian the Widow, Petronella daughter of Howel, and several women with odd names: Rosa Cras ('the Hoarse') and Elena Puke.

If a few women have odd names, some men had really extraordinary ones in addition to the Gobeyonds and the Gotobeds. Most are clearly nicknames, though not all: Mile Pelle, Sicoth, Duys, Magekyn, Germanus Dru, Bola Hardy, Mab Bras, Mab Tal, Ieuan ap Alkoc. Then as well as Moelgoch we have Cloffyn, the lame man known only by that title, William Cas ('nasty Will'). There are more occupational names: William le Verriour (was he a glazier?), Ithel Saer, the craftsman, David the smith, Llewelyn Cais the constable, and Einion Pysgotwr, the fisherman.

Then there are some names which resonate. John Scudamore, the constable himself, whom we saw paying for two burgages, appears in the court roll, as does John of St David's, whom it is known from other sources was the castle's storekeeper in the 1320s. Unlike William the Janitor, he was a complainant, not an accused. Adam of Llangorwen is named, possibly the first appearance in writing of that place-name. A rare personal name is that of Llawdden. There is a strong local association here; a twelfth-century Llawdden is known in Bartrum's pedigrees as a local gentry ancestor figure; his descendants are named by Deio ap Ieuan Du in his poetic peregrination through the county:

Enwaf y cwmwd einym	*I name our own commote,*
Perfedd, diomedd, da ym.	*Perfedd, undeniable, good to me.*
Llawdden oedd y gwarden gynt	*Llawdden was once its warden*
(hil Llawdden hael oll oeddynt).	*(Llawdden of generous family).*

Llawdden also occurs as a local place-name at Rhosllawdden (Capel Madog), and Neuadd Lawdden, the original name of Nanteos. The Llawdden of 1301 is named several times in rather obscure contexts: 'Of David ab Ieuan for the pledge of Llawdden ab Ieuan', paying threepence. Bartrum's patriarchal Llawdden Hen is dated earlier than this court roll, but he is located in Uwch Aeron, and according to Bartrum a Llawdden ap Ieuan was one of his descendants.

Then there's a man called Gwallog, which makes us think immediately of Wallog mansion north of Clarach, and of the legendary figure of Gwallog ap Lleënawg – Hairy son of Literate. Even more intriguing, by contrast, is the name of Richard Lamley – could this possibly be the name Lumley which still survives in the town? Alas, it seems most unlikely, or the name would probably have appeared in the 1543 Lay Subsidy roll, which is another interesting Aberystwyth document – but beyond the scope of this brief essay.

Making Waves

Fflur Dafydd

In Aberystwyth, the night comes at you in huge black waves. I remember sitting by the bay windows of the Bay Hotel, the Glengower, or maybe even the dearly-departed Seabank Hotel, wondering whether those waves were really as distant as they seemed. I imagined it several times: the gushes of foam sashaying through the doors, the swirl of water topping up and toppling our drinks, the night washing our reflections away while we clung to the life-raft of our tables, a feisty-few still playing tippit. To live in Aberystwyth is to face such possibilities, night after night. It is to face the world through a dark glass, knowing that the glass separates that which is undecidedly real and that which is decidedly unreal, the tempest without and the tempest within.

In Aberystwyth, time traverses through a series of unsuitable houses and random streets. Ours was the student Aberystwyth of the late-nineties, which looks now, in frayed photographs, like the nineties-that-was-so-eighties. It was the very precipice from which we looked out over the strange unfathomable depths of a new millennium. Our stance is positively apocalyptic; the hair in uneven tufts around our heads, our clothes a melange of pale yellows and chequered browns, the odd bright turquoise bursting forth from one who dared to be different; trousers a subtle flare around tattered shoes. Ours were the long, interconnecting lanes of Pantycelyn, John

Williams and the Student Village, which spurt forth into the labyrinthine paths linking Scholars, Rummers, the Coopers Arms, The Pier Hotel, the Boar's Head, The Mill, Pipers, The Upper Limit, the Commodore, Lord Beechings, Pier Video, Laura Place, Penglais Hill, the Llandinam Building and Hugh Owen Library, with some journeys encompassing all fifteen destinations for the price of one, like some student-savvy Spartacus baguette-combo. Along the way there were certain detours; alleyways that needed to be darted into, hedges that could be crawled under, ruins to be ruminated upon, a sea occasionally dipped into with a hesitant toe, but at the end of each journey, we always found ourselves at the very core of the maze, alone, calling out one another's names. Later on, the maze narrowed a little, and we found ourselves committing to certain streets more than others. First there was Stanley Road and its crazy paving, its seagull-infested windowsills, the beds that dipped in the middle, a party that kept on happening, a Fellini-film of a third floor. Then, there was North Road and its big, roomy, Victorian house, its windows overlooking the bowling-green, a cellar that was exclusively for physical-theatre-gatherings, and a street full of lax dog owners which cost us a fortune in new trainers.

In Aberystwyth, one experiences intoxication that is impossible to replicate. There's no greater substance than daily lungfuls of sea air, intensifying any other experience that comes your way. There is the wonderful, green abandon of hurling yourself into the bushes by the Porter's Lodge. There are the hungover mornings when doors have been broken, phone boxes have been redecorated, bacon has been thrown onto the walls, when two men fight over who gets to wear your vintage tennis dress for the clean-up operation. There is the evening that brings you the homeless man in a hat, who claims that the previous night you gave him your address and promised him cake (which your flatmate then has to bake). There is finding yourself in the strangest houses, clinging on to the night with your fingertips, dressed in a bright yellow fleece which lights up the room like a beacon. There is a tree-tall man, who picks you up outside Pier Pressure (because you're hiccupping) and runs half way down the prom with you on his shoulder, your friends shouting in the distance. He

puts you down and asserts proudly that it's the perfect remedy. You hiccup into his face.

To live in Aberystwyth is to see all these things, again and again, playing on a screen in a shop window the next day, because some strange man insists on filming these blue-lit nights spilling into red-eyed mornings. He says it's his calling.

In Aberystwyth, it is possible to get stuck upside down, dangling from a great height, and see the world differently. One night (the night I was supposed to be revising for a Medieval Literature exam), I was persuaded by a procrastinating friend to go to the fair. One of the fair rides broke, leaving thirty-two fair-goers stranded in mid-air. I saw the National Library as I had never seen it before. It made sense to me that way up, crowned by light, its long face looming into the sky. By the time I'd been hoisted back out of the ride, the world looked plain ordinary. I'd had an awakening; I'd seen Aberystwyth as I thought it was meant to be seen, from a completely different angle, its core disappearing into the darkness. Four of us walked home that night with the blood rushing back to our legs, the world trying to steady itself on its confused feet. I felt different, relieved, exhilarated. The next morning the *Cambrian News* and *Tivy Side* were battling it out for the exclusive: 'Students tell of terror fair ordeal'. Some fair-goers said they'd had panic attacks, some were taken to hospital for shock, some had nightmares. When they asked me how I felt I told them I'd had an epiphany. 'Sounds nasty,' the reporter said.

In Aberystwyth, epiphanies keep on happening. Time came at me in a flock of birds when I was walking around the corner from the Old College towards the sea. What the birds were doing that night seemed unreal somehow, the swathes of black patterns across the sky pulling time apart, sliding the world from underneath itself in soft angles, a rush of feather and air. All I know is for that one moment I was left reeling, the world upside down again, the sky lavender-lather at my feet. Never have I since felt that tug of nature that came to me then, those birds pulling me away from myself as I rounded the corner by Pen Roc. I've searched, in vain, for the same feeling ever since.

It is possible to try to relive Aberystwyth, with the strangest results. In 2004 I

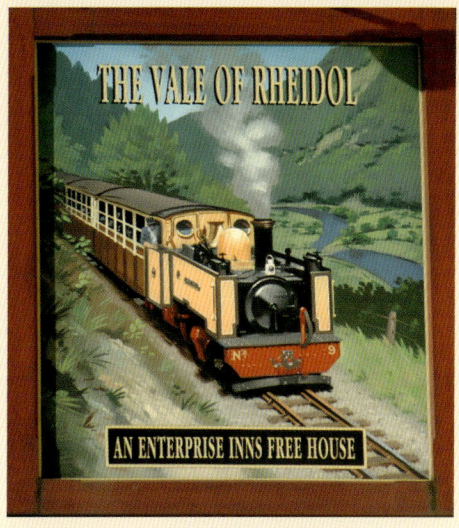

came back for three months, to finish my doctorate. I was only five years away from my undergraduate experience, but I may as well have been a decade away. I committed myself to a wardrobe of a room in Brynderw Hall, sharing with Japanese flatmates who stayed out all night, came back at 7am, and broke the toilet seat on a nightly basis. I only possessed one plastic bowl, a fork, and some shower gel. I roamed the streets, looking for old friends, old haunts; neither seemed to be there any more, even though the same jazz band played at the bandstand, the saxophonist reeling out the same jokes in between exhalations. I saw ghosts of my former self at every street corner: smoking at the corner of Portland Street, falling over outside the Angel, muttering to myself all the way from Great Darkgate Street to South Beach, banging on a door on Thespian Street until my knuckles hurt. I would trace these figures and they'd be gone; it would be this new, rootless self staring back at me, from the door of a pub I'd never seen before.

In Aberystwyth, silence is always changing. During my revisit, I spent every day in the National Library, having the same conversations with the same library-goers at the same doorstop each morning; though the silence of the North Reading Room was always new. I stayed there from half past nine till six in the evening, and there was none of the nonchalance of the undergraduate in me, who flounced out at the slightest excuse, into the sunshine, leaving the books to keep arriving at the table for no one. Until, that is, the day I was persuaded by the very same procrastinating friend (who happened to be passing through) to take an afternoon off and spend it at the Pier, squandering loose change in the arcade. Instead of studying R.S. Thomas's *The Echoes Return Slow* I watched my shining ten pences ebbing away beneath the glass, a silver tide of no return.

To revisit Aberystwyth is to see how the place changes, without its inhabitants really noticing. That is the true way to experience Aberystwyth, right at its core, its change becoming your change. The people who have chosen to stay are the most contented. Every time I visit Aber I always see the same man. Without fail. I don't know his name, have no clue what he does, have never spoken to him, but I recognise him as the face of Aberystwyth. He's there as some testament that there is something

deep and unchanging at the heart of the town, that some features are destined to remain. And it was because *my* features were different, because *I'd* changed, that Aber was no longer the same place. Too many other places had claimed me. Bangor, Beaumaris, Bardsey, Helsinki, Swansea. I'd begun making waves across other coastlines. I'd not been faithful.

To live in Aberystwyth is to treasure the tiny memories, over and over again, in colossal locations. Above North Road, there is a bluebell field that seems wholly untouched, wholly separate from the town. I once walked there with a friend, the bowing blue heads the only witnesses to our conversation. A little higher again is Ynys Las, where I once parked in a car, and cried, sat next to a man who said he had never cried, ever. At one corner of Marine Terrace is a shop where I used to go and buy ginger beer on a Sunday, a corner that seems to me, even now, to trap a peculiar shade of sunlight that can't be found anywhere else. There is a particular telephone box on Northgate Street that I used to telephone my mother when, breathless and ecstatic, I had some good news to give her. There is the old Market Hall where so many of my Saturday mornings were spent, conversing with a woman who wore fingerless gloves and had a kind, peachy face, who encouraged me to buy the most ridiculous outfits which were never worn. There is Constitution Hill and its many velvet black nights; a tryst on a deserted deck, the words being hurled out to sea.

To live in Aberystwyth is to learn to love the uphill struggle and the downhill dawdle. You learn to love the huff and puff of Penglais Hill, and there is a determination deep within that keeps the students puffing, the cyclists cycling, and the long-haul lorries shuddering. Because the arduous ascent is also indelibly linked to the liberating descent that follows. In front of you stand the boasting tips of the Old College, the peaks of centuries floating there as if suspended on the water, a seaside town rising out of the blue, shimmering like a mirage in the distance. Your legs, on the way down, are almost a separate entity; charging on towards the glittering possibilities.

In Aberystwyth, many things are a mirage. Once you're on North Parade, flowing into Great Darkgate Street and into the thick of it, you become the mass itself;

indistinguishable, part of the redbrick, the concrete, the vast expanse of blue, your voice united with the squeal of the seagulls. The picture-postcard slither of Penglais Hill is already a distant memory, and you realise that it's only when you tower above the place that you see what is really there; which is a bit like dangling upside-down above the town, held in the clutches of a fairground ride. It's only then that you truly see that the sea isn't really the sea at all; it's the sky.

And with the world turned on its head at this strange angle, you know you're in Aberystwyth.

Knowledge capital

Andrew Green

Nothing is quite what it seems here. Take its name: Aberystwyth. Anyone with a basic knowledge of Welsh etymology might expect the town to be found clustered in the broad plain of the river Ystwyth, behind Tan-y-bwlch beach. Instead, it lies close to the mouth of another river altogether, the Rheidol. So Aber-rheidol should be its name. In fact the real Aberystwyth does exist, reduced and forgotten, above woodland on a ridge half a mile from the sea: the remains of a ringwork and bailey fortification, Tanycastell. It was built not by the megalomaniac Edward I who was responsible for Aber-rheidol's stone castle, but by an earlier Norman carpetbagger, Gilbert de Clare, in 1110.

A little historical knowledge is useful in this town. Take another example of things not being what they seem: the Old College on the seafront. It looks just like a hotel. And it was designed to be just that, by the wildly optimistic Victorian entrepreneur Thomas Savin. He nurtured fantasies about thousands of well-heeled holidaymakers flocking to Aber from Shrewsbury on the newly opened railway. It's pleasing to think that, since the University now wishes to sell it, it could revert to being an eccentric hotel – just as the theological college next door, originally a hotel, has become 'The Cambrian', with a restaurant and rooms.

Here are some more oddities. What appears to be (and was) the railway station turns out to be a JW Wetherspoon's pub. 'The Academy', which might suggest to the unwary a learned branch of the University, occupies the former St Paul's Welsh Wesleyan chapel, its pulpit and pious murals mocked by the barrels and wine glasses. Meanwhile, the Coliseum theatre long ago transmuted into the town's museum, Castell Brychan promotes books instead of Catholicism, and the new police station is a mock castle.

It's perhaps no coincidence that the town boasts two institutions that celebrate the deception of first visual impressions. One of Aber's most recent buildings is the visualisation centre on the University campus: from the outside an unremarkable white building, on the inside a factory of illusion, where raw data are transmuted into 3-D images of suns, bridges and cars. The other is the camera obscura on the top of Constitution Hill, the world's largest, according to its guardians. Here you can peer down on the town, changed from its normal strangeness into something even stranger. (To complete the picture the authorities have taken to floodlighting the slopes of Constitution Hill in a strange orange glow: a spectral and shocking sight, even to those who have lived here for years.)

I first came to live in Aber in August 1973. The heat was oppressive. I was set to work in a room at the front of the Old College, and wondered why I'd come. Why, I thought, looking out of the window, was Thomas Savin convinced that he could entice families to a resort with no sand, just a bayful of grey grit? I found the town threatening. All those Victorian terrace houses, none with enough light. My landlady in Bath Street was Mrs Jones. She said little (but then so did I as a callow youth), and always watched the wrestling on television on Saturday afternoon. When she did talk she spoke Welsh: I felt at a disadvantage. A greyness seemed to lie over the whole town. Chapels dominated almost every street; some, like Tabernacl, lorded it over whole districts. Sundays, when nothing opened and nothing happened, were insufferable. Even today, with Calvinism in headlong retreat, Aber seems not to know how to enjoy itself on Sunday: hedonism doesn't come naturally to people here, as it does in, say, Tenby or Swansea.

Gradually, though, I found my way around. The town became more familiar, and I even stayed a second year, admittedly in Llanbadarn. Here Victorian values held less sway, perhaps under the influence still of Dafydd ap Gwilym (if he were alive today he would ogle the girls in Morrison's instead of in the church).

I didn't return to live in the town for 22 years. When I did, the changes, for good and sometimes ill, were obvious. Colour had invaded the town. Social mores had loosened, partly thanks to the University's expansion. Drunken shouts had replaced the former biblical silence of the streets. Welsh-language culture was broader-based, and the attitudes of non-Welsh speakers to it healthier. Hip independent shops have opened, and share the centre with determined survivors of another age, like the National Milk Bar, recently the subject of a scholarly article. The out-of-town retail sheds, by contrast, are depressingly similar to those in other towns, and just as destructive. The Rheidol's flood plain has been built on, in time to receive the next floods.

Other things haven't changed. Aber is still geographically remote, its road and rail links as tenuous as ever: in very bad weather the town can get cut off from the outside world. More serious is the mental distance outsiders construct to protect themselves from the temptation to visit. This is not all bad. At one of the many meetings I've attended at which this topic was discussed a police officer remarked that it was Aber's very remoteness that was to thank for the fact that locking your car or even your house was less necessary here than in the vast majority of UK police areas. Not that you'd guess that this was true from reading the novels of Niall Griffiths or Malcolm Pryce. Though of course the effects they create derive in large part from the patent ridiculousness of violent crime or wizardry on Aber's streets (which is not to deny that Aber has its share of social problems).

For all its remoteness the town has long possessed a surprisingly international character. In large part the University is responsible. Since 1872, and in spite of its slow, shaky start and small scale, it has always insisted on a worldwide outlook. It never ceases to amaze outsiders that the first Chair of International Politics in the world was created in Aber, in 1919, and named after the US President Woodrow

Wilson. The Department of International Politics continues to have the reputation of being one of the leading university politics departments in the world. I'm no longer surprised when I meet eminent librarians in Asia and Africa and hear them speak warmly about their studies in the pioneering College of Librarianship Wales, now the Department of Information Studies. The Plant Breeding Station, now IGER and shortly to move into the University, gained an early international reputation for its work, thanks to the genius of Sir George Stapledon.

Some of the town's links with other countries are odder. In the 1920s its leaders formed a curious relationship with a sculptor from Rome, Mario Rutelli. He is best known for creating the bronze figure of a near naked girl as the centrepiece of the seafront war memorial, unveiled in 1923. Why the normally well-buttoned aldermen should have taken leave of their senses and commissioned such an unrestrained and unprotestant image is not clear. Rutelli completed three other sculptures for the town: the stolid and disappointing statue of Sir John Williams for the main Reading Room of the National Library, a sprightly pixie balanced on a globe as a monument for the dead of Tabernacl Chapel in Powell Street, and, in front of the Old College, the only public statue in existence of King Edward VIII: a young man with a confident pose and a confident gaze, betraying nothing of the troubles that led to decades of exile and ignominy.

Somehow these global links coexist with an extreme localism. Aber's social conversations take place in a network of fiercely exclusive but always locally owned cafés: the Penguin, the Cabin, Caffi Morgan, the Blue Creek and the rest. Local, that is, until recently. A few months ago a branch of Costa Coffee (owner Whitbread plc, revenue in 2007-08 £98.1m) opened in Great Darkgate Street. Protestors immediately gathered outside, angry that a multinational company had offended against bilingualism, locally sourced produce and (allegedly) the planning rules. These were no doubt some of the same dissenters who came out on the streets five years before to protest against an event of truly international significance: the decision of a duplicitous government to send troops to war in Iraq. Local and global on the same banner.

Cross Trefechan Bridge to the mouth of the Rheidol and similar kinds of contrasts meet you. Trefechan was historically a poor and unhygienic part of town – its nickname was 'Turkey' – but in recent years it has been made more respectable by the addition of flats and government offices. Small fishing boats still sail from the harbour – though most of the lobsters they bring in are wheeled away in pantechnicons to southern Europe. But in the 1990s the harbour was redesignated a marina. Working boats are far outnumbered by pleasure craft, although many of these never leave their berths and seem to be an excuse for pottering rather than serious sport.

From the window of my room in the National Library I look out on all these paradoxes and contrasts in the town below. But if I turn back from the window I have to admit that what marks Aber as special for me is not the individual small wonders of the town, but a greater wonder, one not immediately obvious to the visitor: the fact that Aber is one of outstanding knowledge capitals of the world.

The town is overlooked by a great temple to knowledge: the National Library of Wales. Temple is an apt metaphor. Its designers consciously aimed at a building that would inspire awe. Nearly a hundred years later its shrine-like image can be off-putting: there are many lifelong residents who have never visited, even though it's a public institution and free to use.

Because of the National Library and similar institutions, like the University, the Welsh Books Council and the Royal Commission on the Ancient and Historical Monuments of Wales, Aber is the focus of a massive concentration of recorded knowledge. No other town in the world, even that medieval miracle Timbuktu, houses more documents per head of population. If we say that the town is home to, very roughly, six million books, that makes about 500 volumes for every single resident.

No national library in the world is situated in such a small place. It's also a perfect example of the local and the universal in harmony. Unusual in providing a completely bilingual service to its readers and visitors, for 100 years it's been seen as a natural home for the Welsh language, as a historical and a living language. The collections it's

best known for – the ancient books and manuscripts, maps, paintings, photographs, records and films – all have Wales and its localities as their subjects. But at the same time it operates internationally. Most of the publications it stores have nothing to do with Wales: they arrive through legal deposit and deal with almost any subject under the sun. Visitors come from all over the world, and the Library has an international reputation for its collections and its specialisms.

An inquisitive person in Aber could never be fully satisfied: there's simply too much to find out, and too much to know.

I'd make a bolder claim: if you were looking for a fertile soil in which to grow a civilized, informed and democratic society there would be fewer more promising places than Aber.

And that's not all. One of the great experiences of Aber is emerging on a spring evening from the National Library after a day's work in its dark interior on to the western terrace. As you blink in the sunlight you see first the slate roofs of the town, then the sweep of Cardigan Bay, and beyond, if you're lucky, a glorious polychrome sunset. It's a prospect hard to replicate anywhere in the world.

This, then, is my Aberystwyth. It's a place that can seem tricky, hard to know and stubbornly local. At the same time it's constantly surprising, cosmopolitan, full of beauties, and unforgettable.

ABER